OXFORD
UNIVERSITY PRESS

Great Clarendon Street, Oxford OX2 6DP
Oxford University Press is a department of the University of Oxford.
It furthers the University's objective of excellence in research, scholarship,
and education by publishing worldwide. Oxford is a registered trade mark of
Oxford University Press in the UK and in certain other countries

British Library Cataloguing in Publication Data

Data available
ISBN: 978-0-19-277262-6

3 5 7 9 10 8 6 4 2

Printed in China

Paper used in the production of this book is a natural,
recyclable product made from wood grown in sustainable forests.
The manufacturing process conforms to the environmental
regulations of the country of origin.

... the **GLORY!**

Team Turbo was the greatest team in Whizz Karts.
Bunny and Bonnie worked together to win the races . . .

It all started after another stunning
victory for Team Turbo.

And they would stop at nothing to get ahead . . .

Bunny **SUPER GLUED** Bonnie's wheels to the race track.

So Bonnie put **ITCHY POWDER** in Bunny's suit.

Then Bunny took Bonnie's kart off charge.

WAH! No power!

And Bonnie filled Bunny's helmet with . . .

SPAGHETTI!

Their teammates had reached the end of the road.

But the bunnies were sure they could win on their own.

FINE!

All they had to do was fix their karts.

How hard could it be?

But they fell asleep before they were finished.

And woke up late for the race!

By the time the bunnies had rolled up, the race had already begun. There was no time to waste.

Together they jumped . . .

The **WHIZZ KART** world held its breath . . .

... but Team Turbo was finally back on track.

And they all agreed that the days of squabbles
and pranks were over ...